WORLD LEADERS

VLADIMIR PUTIN

PRESIDENT OF RUSSIA

by Michael Regan

www.focusreaders.com

Focus Readers is distributed by North Star Editions:
sales@northstareditions.com | 888-417-0195

Produced for Focus Readers by Red Line Editorial.

Content Consultant: Andrew Jenks, Professor of History, California State University, Long Beach

Photographs ©: Felipe Dana/AP Images, cover, 1; AP Images, 4–5; svic/Shutterstock Images, 7; RIA Novosti/Sputnik/AP Images, 8–9; Red Line Editorial, 10, 31; dade72/Shutterstock Images, 13; mutee meesa/Shutterstock Images, 15; Berliner Verlag/Archiv/picture-alliance/dpa/AP Images, 16–17; Valentin Baranovskiy/Sputnik/AP Images, 19; Boris Yurchenko/AP Images, 20–21; Everett Historical/ Shutterstock Images, 23; Julia Rumyantseva/Shutterstock Images, 25; Popova Valeriya/Shutterstock Images, 26–27; Ivan Sekretarev/AP Images, 29, 35; STR/STR/EPA Pool/AP Images, 32–33; Alexander Zemlianichenko/AP Images, 37, 42; Northfoto/Shutterstock Images, 39; Sergey Guneev/Sputnik/AP Images, 40–41; Kyodo/AP Images, 45

ISBN
978-1-63517-551-6 (hardcover)
978-1-63517-623-0 (paperback)
978-1-63517-767-1 (ebook pdf)
978-1-63517-695-7 (hosted ebook)

Library of Congress Control Number: 2017948126

Printed in the United States of America
Mankato, MN
November, 2017

ABOUT THE AUTHOR

Michael Regan worked as a community college and university career counselor before turning his attention to research and writing. He is especially interested in topics related to technology and current events. In his spare time, he enjoys watercolor painting, hiking, tai chi, and reading. He lives in southern Arizona with his spouse and two cats.

TABLE OF CONTENTS

CHAPTER 1

A SUBMARINE SINKS

On August 12, 2000, newly elected Russian President Vladimir Putin went on vacation. Early the next morning, he received a call from Russia's minister of defense. Russia's newest nuclear submarine, the *Kursk*, had sunk. It was designed to battle US aircraft carriers. However, a torpedo in the bow of the ship had misfired. Many of the 113 people on board died immediately.

The explosion that occurred in the Barents Sea was felt as far away as Alaska.

But 23 sailors had survived in a back compartment. They waited to be rescued.

The Russian commanders did not tell Putin the truth at first. They told him the submarine was missing. Several days later, the Russian navy admitted to the explosion. They blamed it on a crash with another submarine. The commanders were more interested in protecting submarine secrets than in saving survivors. Putin continued his vacation.

Other countries offered to send help, but Putin refused. US President Bill Clinton finally persuaded Putin to accept help. Within six hours of arriving on the scene, British and Norwegian divers were able to open the submarine's hatch. The Russians had failed at the task for nine days. Because of the delay, those waiting to be rescued had died.

The control room of the *Kursk* was preserved as a monument in Murmansk, Russia.

A Russian TV station criticized Putin for not acting faster. The owner of the station, Boris Berezovsky, had once been Putin's mentor. But Putin accused the channel of lying about him. He ordered investigations into Berezovsky's past financial dealings. Berezovsky fled the country to avoid arrest.

Eventually, Putin took control of the television station. He knew he could use the media to shape a positive image of himself. By the end of his first year in office, Putin controlled Russia's three major television stations.

CHAPTER 2

RUSSIA THEN AND NOW

The nation that Vladimir Putin leads has existed only since 1991. Prior to that, Russia was part of the Soviet Union. This nation was formed in 1922 after **Communists** won a bloody civil war.

For decades, the Soviet Union was the most powerful Communist country in the world. Vladimir Lenin was the country's first leader. He controlled the republics of the Soviet Union. Russia was the largest of these republics.

Vladimir Lenin was the founder of the Russian Communist Party.

When Lenin died in 1924, Joseph Stalin became the Soviet Union's leader. Under Stalin's rule, **industrialization** increased. However, food production decreased. Eventually, the country

REPUBLICS OF THE SOVIET UNION

ESTONIA

LATVIA

LITHUANIA

BELARUS

UKRAINE

MOLDOVA

GEORGIA

ARMENIA

AZERBAIJAN

RUSSIA

KAZAKHSTAN

UZBEKISTAN

TURKMENISTAN

TAJIKISTAN

KYRGYZSTAN

N

W E

S

could not provide enough food for its citizens. During the winter of 1932 to 1933, millions of people starved to death. Even so, Stalin kept his focus on the country's military efforts.

Under Stalin's rule, the Soviet Union became a major military power. During World War II (1939–1945), Germany suffered 75 percent of its losses fighting the Soviet Union. Despite the nation's military success, Soviet citizens did not have much freedom. They could be arrested and killed for criticizing Communism. Estimates of deaths caused by Stalin's rule vary. Some experts believe the number was more than 20 million.

In the Soviet Union, all goods and services were **centralized**. That way, citizens would have equal access to things such as food, health care, and jobs. But in reality, some Soviets were much richer than others.

The Soviet government placed small groups of businessmen in charge of major industries. These included mining, construction, energy production, agriculture, transportation, and the military. Industry leaders became powerful and wealthy.

In 1985, Mikhail Gorbachev rose to power. He wanted to give more freedom to Soviet citizens. He restructured the country, taking power away from Communist party leaders. Some Communists disagreed with the changes. In 1991, government and military officials tried to overthrow Gorbachev's government. Though the attempt failed, it weakened Gorbachev as a leader. He resigned in December of that year, and the Soviet government crumbled.

After the collapse of the Soviet Union, 11 of the country's 15 republics claimed independence.

The Russian president's official residence in Moscow, Russia, is known as the Kremlin.

Boris Yeltsin was elected the new president of Russia. Similar to Gorbachev, Yeltsin moved the nation away from Communism and toward **democracy**. Many members of the old Soviet political structure lost their positions.

FOCUS ON
RUSSIA

Russia has the largest surface area of any nation in the world. The country extends from eastern Europe, across northern Asia, to the Pacific Ocean. The eastern tip of Russia is less than 55 miles (89 km) from the US state of Alaska. The massive nation is home to more than 142 million people. Its capital is Moscow.

Russia's two major religions are Christianity and Islam. The country's official language is Russian. Most of Russia's wealth comes from its oil and natural gas resources.

According to the country's 1993 constitution, Russia is a federal semi-presidential republic. In this system, a president and prime minister share power. The president is elected by the public, and the prime minister is appointed by the president.

1941–1945: More than 10 million Soviet soldiers die during World War II.

December 1991: The Soviet Union falls, and Russia becomes an independent state.

December 31, 1999: Boris Yeltsin resigns as president and appoints Vladimir Putin in his place.

March 26, 2000: Putin is elected president of Russia for the first time.

February–May 2014: Russian forces take over Crimea, a region of Ukraine.

CHAPTER 3

EARLY YEARS AND FAMILY LIFE

Vladimir Putin was born in Leningrad, Russia, in 1952. The city is now known as Saint Petersburg. Vladimir was the only child in a poor family. His father oversaw workers in a metal factory. Vladimir's family had to share an apartment with two other families.

From first to fifth grade, Vladimir was a troublemaker at school. He was always late to class. He wasn't interested in studying, either.

Putin's parents survived the German invasion of Leningrad in World War II.

However, during sixth grade, Vladimir's grades improved. He became more involved in school and joined sports. He started making goals for himself. One of his goals was to someday join the KGB, Russia's security agency. His interest in spy movies likely influenced this goal.

Vladimir's grades continued to improve. He was able to enter a respected high school. He also became skilled in the martial arts of sambo and jiujitsu. Sambo is a Russian sport that combines judo and wrestling. Despite being small, Vladimir was tough. By age 16, he was a top-ranked expert at sambo.

> # ➤ THINK ABOUT IT

What are some ways Vladimir's early years might have influenced his future role as a world leader?

Leningrad State University later became Saint Petersburg State University, one of the top schools in Russia.

After high school, Putin entered Leningrad State University. He graduated with a law degree in 1975. He then fulfilled one of his long-term goals by taking a job with the KGB.

Putin married Lyudmila Shkrebneva in 1983. He had met her three years earlier, when she was working as a flight attendant. The couple had two daughters. Maria, called Masha, was born in 1985. Yekaterina, known as Katerina, was born in 1986.

CHAPTER 4

COMING TO POWER

In 1975, Putin was the only person in his graduating class chosen for the KGB. His first assignment was to **recruit** foreigners to spy for the Soviet Union. In the 1980s, Putin was transferred to Dresden, East Germany. He worked undercover as Mr. Adamov, the director of a German–Soviet social club. Putin's actual work in Dresden was never revealed to the public.

The KGB headquarters featured a banner of Lenin during a Communist Party conference in 1988.

He most likely gathered secret information for the Soviet government.

Putin had his first taste of power at the Soviet intelligence headquarters in Dresden. One night in 1989, an angry mob surrounded the building. The East German government had announced the end of the Berlin Wall a few weeks earlier. For years, the wall had prevented travel between East Germany and West Germany. With the border open, protesters of the East German government could freely roam the streets.

Putin called Moscow for help, but government leaders told him he was on his own. He started burning secret KGB documents. Then, he told the mob that armed guards were inside. The mob broke up, and Putin was safe. But according to one journalist, the experience scared Putin. He developed a fear of popular **uprising**.

The Berlin Wall separated families and restricted East Germans' freedom.

In 1990, Putin returned to Leningrad. The city was renamed Saint Petersburg a year later. Putin retired from the KGB and became an adviser to Anatoly Sobchak. Sobchak was the first democratically elected mayor of Saint Petersburg.

Both Sobchak and Putin had supported Mikhail Gorbachev's changes during the mid-1980s. They hoped the changes would strengthen the Soviet Union as a global power. The goal was to reach the same status as the United States, Japan, and Germany.

Sobchak promoted Putin to first deputy major in 1994. Under Sobchak and Putin's leadership, Saint Petersburg built highways, **telecommunication** services, and hotels. Major foreign companies began opening offices in the city as well.

Sobchak lost reelection in 1996. A year later, Putin joined Russian President Boris Yeltsin's circle of advisors. Putin was promoted to secretary of the Russian Security Council within two years. The Security Council advised the president on national security, foreign policy, law

▲ Today, many people consider Saint Petersburg to be the cultural capital of Russia.

enforcement, and the military. Putin's political

career was on the rise.

CHAPTER 5

PUTIN REBUILDS RUSSIA

The Russian **parliament**, called the State Duma, held a meeting in August 1999. The leaders were meeting to approve President Yeltsin's recommendation for prime minister. This was Yeltsin's fifth recommendation in 16 months. He had fired the previous four. One Duma leader could not even remember the new candidate's name. The leaders listened to the candidate's speech and approved him for the position.

The Russian parliament meets in the State Duma Building in Moscow.

It was official. Russia's new prime minister was Vladimir Putin.

Just a month after Putin's appointment, four apartment buildings in Russia were bombed. The source of the bombings was unknown. But Putin blamed the Chechens. Chechnya was a small republic that had broken away from Russia in the mid-1990s. The two nations were in a years-long conflict. Putin reacted to the bombings by taking a strong stance against terrorism.

Putin's handling of the attacks brought him greater attention. When Yeltsin resigned in December 1999, he appointed Putin as acting president. Putin was prepared for the job. He had plans to rebuild a country that was close to collapse.

Just one year earlier, Russia had not been able to pay its debts. Public workers were paid late

Nearly 300 people died in the 1999 Moscow apartment bombings.

or not at all. Outside of Saint Petersburg, the country's roads and bridges were falling apart. And most of Russia's wealth belonged to a few industry leaders.

Putin aimed to restore Russian stability. He also intended to rebuild the country's world status. To do so, he would enforce basic order within the country.

Because of Putin's secretive KGB background, the rest of the world knew little about him. In his first speech as acting president, Putin tried to appeal to other governments. He promised freedom of speech and religion. He also promised to protect citizens' right to private property.

In March 2000, Putin was elected president of Russia. His leadership was now official. However, Putin's first years as president saw many challenges. In August 2000, the *Kursk* sank. In 2002, Chechen rebels attacked a theater in Moscow. More than 130 hostages died. Many of the deaths were caused by gas that Russian forces pumped into the theater.

Despite these tragedies, Putin stayed popular with the public. He was elected to another term in 2004. Meanwhile, gas and oil prices were on the rise. Sales of these goods gave the Russian government large amounts of money. As a result, Putin had more resources to carry out his plans.

By 2008, Russia was able to pay all its debts. Average incomes rose, and unemployment fell. Some critics said Putin was simply in the right place at the right time. Still, many Russian people saw Putin as a wise and effective leader.

THE PRESIDENT COMPARED TO THE PRIME MINISTER IN RUSSIA ◁

President's Powers

► Leads Russia and the armed forces
► Controls foreign planning
► Appoints the prime minister
► Signs or vetoes laws by the Russian legislature
► Controls the Russian Security Council
► Can call states of emergency

Prime Minister's Powers

► Leads the cabinet of ministers
► Carries out foreign planning
► Creates economic and budget plans
► Sets gas, electric, and transport prices
► Controls social and labor plans
► Serves as acting president if necessary

CHAPTER 6

CHALLENGES AT HOME AND ABROAD

Early in his presidency, Putin appeared to be focused on making the world a safer place. In 2002, Russia and the United States agreed to reduce their possession of nuclear weapons. That same year, Russia and the North Atlantic Treaty Organization (NATO) created a group to discuss security threats.

Putin also wanted a more stable state. To do so, he took greater control of the Chechen conflict.

US President George W. Bush visited Putin in 2002 to discuss efforts against terrorism.

Putin began labeling Chechen independence fighters as terrorists. That way, Russian citizens and leaders would not criticize Putin's actions against Chechnya.

In 2004, armed attackers targeted a school in the Russian region of North Ossetia. Approximately 330 people died. More than half of the victims were children. Putin blamed the attack on terrorists who were connected to Chechnya. He used the attack as a reason to increase security in Russia.

Putin continued to gain power by eliminating the elections for regional governors. Instead, the positions would be appointed by the central government. Putin also appointed his friends to powerful industry positions.

Meanwhile, Putin's government took control of railroads, construction, high-tech industries,

△ People lay flowers on a monument honoring the victims of the 2004 school attack.

banking, energy production, and the media. These actions caused criticism from around the world. Russian citizens and world leaders accused Putin's government of **corruption**. One Russian politician said that corruption in Russia had become a way of life.

In February 2014, Russia's relations with other major nations declined rapidly. Russian forces had invaded Crimea, which was a part of Ukraine.

The invasion was Russia's largest conflict with Western nations since the Soviet Union's collapse. The United States and its allies in Europe criticized Putin's actions.

Russia's relationship with the United States took another hit in 2016. US intelligence groups accused Putin of interfering in the US presidential election. Many experts believed Putin wanted to sway voters toward candidate Donald Trump. However, Putin denied any Russian involvement.

Meanwhile in Russia, falling wages and rising food prices caused citizen complaints. For the last several years, oil prices had fallen, and trade with

> ## THINK ABOUT IT

What do you think causes corruption in businesses and governments?

Protestors in Moscow carry Ukrainian and Russian flags to protest Putin's actions in Crimea.

Western nations had suffered. Russia was facing an economic crisis. In some ways, Putin had succeeded in rebuilding the country of his youth. However, this meant many old problems were still not fixed.

FOCUS ON
DMITRY MEDVEDEV

In Russia, the president cannot serve more than two terms in a row. That meant Putin could not run for a third term in 2008. But Putin did not want to lose power. He needed the next president to make him prime minister. To ensure this, Putin supported Dmitry Medvedev for president in the 2008 election.

Medvedev had worked closely with Putin in the past. In 2000, Medvedev ran Putin's election campaign for president of Russia. Putin rewarded him for his work. He appointed Medvedev the head of Russia's natural gas industry.

Medvedev was elected president in 2008. He immediately named Putin prime minister. Medvedev spoke a lot about change, but little of his agenda came true. He did not have as much power as Putin. This made it difficult

In March 2017, Dmitry Medvedev (left) had an approval rating of only 42 percent.

for him to push items through the Russian parliament. Medvedev's greatest accomplishment was Russia's entrance into the World Trade Organization (WTO). The WTO is an international group that oversees trade between nations.

Just before the end of his four-year term, Medvedev resigned. He named Putin acting president. In 2012, Putin was elected president for the third time. Once in office, he appointed Medvedev prime minister.

CHAPTER 7

PUTIN'S ROLES IN RUSSIA

Despite an economic decline, Putin remains popular in Russia. In 2017, Putin had an 83 percent approval rating. Russians between the ages of 18 and 24 were even more supportive. Putin's popularity soared when Russia took over Crimea. Many young Russians equate military strength with greatness. They are proud of their country, despite its economic struggles.

Putin poses with young athletes at a Russian ice hockey school.

Putin (center) and citizens celebrate the 72nd anniversary of Russia's victory in World War II.

Rebuilding Russian pride was one of Putin's goals as president. He wanted other nations to admire Russia. He also wanted Russian citizens to admire their own country. To achieve this, Putin demanded loyalty to the state.

Putin's ideas of state loyalty often went against democratic principles. According to Putin, only the state could create order in a nation. Changes should be carried out by the government, not by the people. This took power away from Russian citizens.

Putin has used his fight against terrorism as a way to build state loyalty. Russia's conflict with Chechnya is an example of this. Putin called Chechens names when they fought for separation from Russia. Since these Chechens weren't loyal to Russia, Putin painted them in a bad light. He called them bandits, terrorists, and scum.

THINK ABOUT IT ◁

How is Putin's idea of Russian pride similar to your idea of patriotism? How is it different?

Some critics think Putin's targeting of Chechens is based on **ethnicity**. However, Putin claims to support Russia's ethnic **minorities**. In a 2013 speech, Putin announced that all Russians must work together to create common goals. He recognized that Russia was built by many ethnic groups. Trying to destroy one group would destroy the whole country. Putin's words gave many Russians hope. But some critics feared that Putin would not follow through.

Rising oil prices and changes made before his presidency brought Putin early success. But some of his success came at the expense of people's freedom. Still, Putin became a symbol of strength to many Russians. He promoted Russian loyalty and spoke out against terrorism. When he first became president, Putin had promised to bring prosperity and security to Russia. He

▲ Putin (left) discussed the importance of Russia's national identity in his September 2013 speech.

also wanted to restore Russia's status as a global power. Despite numerous controversies, Putin has fulfilled those promises.

FOCUS ON
VLADIMIR PUTIN

Write your answers on a separate piece of paper.

1. Write a one-paragraph summary of one of Putin's challenges in office.

2. Do you think Russia is a true democracy? Why or why not?

3. What is the name of the Russian parliament?
    - **A.** Chechnya
    - **B.** Kursk
    - **C.** State Duma

4. What would be likely to happen if a government controlled all media in a country?
    - **A.** Only bad stories about the government would be reported.
    - **B.** Only good stories about the government would be reported.
    - **C.** Information would be more accurate.

Answer key on page 48.

GLOSSARY

centralized
Controlled by a single authority.

Communists
People who belong to a political party that believes the government should own all property.

corruption
Dishonest or illegal acts, especially by powerful people.

democracy
A system of government in which the people have power. Democracy typically involves elections.

ethnicity
National or cultural characteristics that connect a group of people.

industrialization
The process in which a country starts manufacturing goods on a large scale.

minorities
Groups of people that make up less than half of a population.

parliament
A group of people who make laws.

recruit
To seek out new members for a group or activity.

telecommunication
Messages sent over cable, radio, or telephone.

uprising
A revolution or rebellion.

TO LEARN MORE

BOOKS

Bearce, Stephanie. *The Cold War.* Waco, TX: Prufrock Press, 2015.

Kenney, Karen Latchana. *What Is Communism?* New York: Gareth Stevens Publishing, 2014.

Uschan, Michael V. *The Central Asian States: Then and Now.* San Diego: ReferencePoint Press, 2015.

NOTE TO EDUCATORS

Visit **www.focusreaders.com** to find lesson plans, activities, links, and other resources related to this title.

INDEX

Answer Key: 1. Answers will vary; **2.** Answers will vary; **3.** C; **4.** B